Contents

4

Foreword

BY HARMONY WALTON

Planning a wedding of any size is no small task. I find the more intimate the gathering, the more important the details – and the photography. As the founder of The Bridal Bar and host of Bridal Bar Radio on iHeartRadio, I've been collaborating on local and destination weddings (and celebrity weddings too) since 2004. I've worked with top talent photographers around the world and I've come to know the importance of a quality team in your corner with a sensibility that mirrors the wedding experience. Rochelle Cheever was one such top photographer that caught my attention early on, and kept it.

Rochelle and I met for the first time in a setting that I would later realize is so fitting of her and her career. Champagne and Aperol Spritz were on the menu at Hotel Hassler, a celebrity-favorite atop the Spanish Steps in Rome, Italy. I had been a big fan of her wedding photography for most of my career and had featured her work on my destination weddings site, Jet Fete. But it would take years before we were in the same city at the same time. As luck would have it, back in 2014 I had the pleasure of meeting Rochelle face-to-face in the eternal city, a place near and dear to my heart and hers. I knew I admired Rochelle's work but it didn't take long for me to admire her as a strong, independent female entrepreneur, too. As an Italian-American, she embodies everything chic and sophisticated about Italy and warm and welcoming about Southern California. We chatted about business, travel, life, and her upcoming move back to San Diego, my hometown, where we would eventually meet again. And ever since that special night in Rome, I am among the lucky who have worked with Rochelle and now call her friend.

Rochelle's sensibility is different from all the rest. Her images have a calming effect to them, much like her demeanor. One of the many reasons she excels in the world of elopement photography. Something so intimate requires a character that can not only capture that closeness, but do so in a way that doesn't impact the event except to elevate it. And she does just that.

In 2017, when Rochelle and I met for coffee in her now home of San Diego, just as her first book was going to print, it became clear she needed to share her vast experience and expertise in elopements with the world. Not long after that, this, her second book was hatched. The Elopement Experience is a visual story of love through many of the intimate events she's captured, paired with her unique perspective, invaluable information, and all the tools needed to help couples plan such a day.

For brides and grooms seeking need-to-know information to elevate their upcoming elopement experience, this book is a must-read. But it's so much more than that. It's a tool to get you down the aisle and an interactive guide to help you design a day that is authentically you. It's packed with tips and expert advice - all paired with imagery that inspires. If you love love like I do, then dive in and allow Rochelle to take you around the world on her clients' journeys. Travel to Rome and back to celebrate brides and grooms expressing that love in a visually captivating way, hopefully leading you to plan a wedding equally as memorable. Learn how to design and plan your own elopement and what to do and where to go, all while enjoying real life inspiration from couples before you who have tied the knot - with just two.

The Elopement Experience is an experience worth partaking in, from cover to cover, eloping or not!

XO
Harmony Walton

Founder of The Bridal Bar + Jet Fete, Host of Bridal Bar Radio

Welcome

Welcome and congratulations on your engagement! If you are planning an elopement, you may be feeling a bit overwhelmed by all the decisions, but no worries. In this book, I'll walk you through the process, helping you with the when, where and what and fine-tuning your choices.

THE ELOPEMENT EXPERIENCE COVERS:

This book is designed to help you prepare for your elopement, with step-by-step advice on determining the type of elopement that's best for you, the perfect location and the ideal time of year. You'll discover a world of exquisite elopement locations, advice on DIY versus wedding planner, the myriad types of elopements, wedding attire, decor and much more.

During the course of a decade spent photographing hundreds of elopements, I have seen what works best and developed a great eye for design, ideal backdrops, and how to choose a venue that is uniquely perfect for each couple.

In this book you'll discover:

+ Types of elopements to choose from

+ Whether you need a wedding planner

+ When to elope

+ Where to elope

+ How to select vendors (hair stylists, makeup, attire, decor, refreshments)

+ How to set up a Pinterest board to gather ideas for your ideal wedding

+ What to pack

You'll find everything you need to begin planning your elopement.

Congratulations to you both!

Rochelle

8

Introduction

Case study: Positano, Civil

Lindsay and Harsh

Venue
Villa Boheme, Positano, Italy

Wedding Planner
DIY

Gown Designer
Katie May

Groom's Clothing Designer
SuitSupply, Gucci

Florist
Flora Garden Aldo

Shoe designer
Jimmy Choo

Jewelry/Rings designer
Cartier, The Mrs. Box

Hair and makeup Artist
Silvia Gerzeli

Catering/Restaurant
Rada

II

What inspired you to choose to do a destination elopement?

While Harsh and I have the same souls, we come from incredibly different cultures. Traditional Indian weddings consist of multiple events and ceremonies over the course of a week, which seemed unnecessarily complicated to us. The thought of planning a modern Christian ceremony combined with a traditional Sikh wedding quickly became overwhelming, so we decided to have an intimate ceremony with the most stunning backdrop.

In what ways did you personalize your wedding day?

Most importantly, we incorporated personalized vows into our Christian wedding ceremony, and hearing my husband's vows was easily my favorite moment of the day. We also included a number of personal details ranging from our wedding monogram designed by our calligrapher, to a hand-dyed French silk ribbon for my bouquet, "Salute" drink stirrers, etc.

What were your favorite wedding day details?

It was quite windy on the day of our wedding, but fortunately the winds subsided just enough for for our boat to depart that afternoon. We took off our shoes and sipped prosecco on the boat deck while cruising along the unbelievably gorgeous Amalfi coastline at sunset. It was a surreal experience, and my husband and I relished the opportunity to reflect on the momentous day. My brother and his girlfriend surprised us with antique crystal goblets from a local shop in Positano, so we loved the significance and history behind our wedding toast.

Was there a particular inspiration or theme behind your elopement?

I worked with calligrapher Heather Brock of Marcardin Calligraphy and Kristin Walker of Twin Ravens Press to design our gold foil pressed wedding announcement. I had a custom wax seal with our monogram created in Hong Kong, and I collected vintage stamps that were symbolic of our home states in New Mexico and California as well as our current home in Texas. My husband and two of my best friends helped line envelopes and assemble each announcement, so the process was truly a group effort.

When I stumbled across Villa Boheme online, I immediately knew that their phenomenal terrace would make the ideal backdrop for our wedding day. I gravitate toward neutral colors, and I planned our wedding theme around gold, cream, and blush. I wanted the day to include subtle nods to Italy without detracting from Positano's natural beauty, so I included marble accents on the wedding announcements as well as olive branches in our floral arrangements.

I found my Katie May dress at a charming boutique in Dallas and was drawn to the timelessness of lace paired with an unexpectedly sexy plunging back line. My dress was also lightweight and did not wrinkle easily, making it perfect for the long haul on an international flight.

Do you have any special advice to share with other brides?

Plan as much as you can in advance, while also focusing on the significance of the moment. So many brides become engulfed in the wedding planning process and allow their stress to detract from the significance of their marriage. International destination weddings involve language barriers amongst many other uncontrollable variables, and it is beneficial to work with vendors who speak the local language and are familiar with the wedding location. Destination brides must be flexible, consider back-up options, and when original plans go awry, laugh it off and realize that regardless of minor mishaps, it is a gift to marry the love of your life

ROCHELLE CHEEVER

13

Chapter 1

Should you elope and why?

THE ELOPEMENT EXPERIENCE

Should You Elope?

Let's start with the basic question: Why Elope? I'm all for elopements, maybe because my own wedding in Rome was an elaborate affair with more than 500 guests, not all of them close personal friends. I was young, only 19, and super shy. I remember being terrified as my Dad and I drove up to the the quaint neighborhood church, which was much too small to accommodate such a large audience. I was dying to run away, not because I didn't want to marry my husband, but because I didn't want to walk down the aisle with all those eyes peering at me.

As a photographer who has spent the past decade specializing in destination weddings, I'm often asked "How can we elope and still make our wedding really memorable?" followed by all sorts of questions about the ideal location, the time of year, time of day — the whole process.

I've photographed well over 200 elopements across the globe, from simple, intimate ceremonies such as a party for two on a wind swept cliff on a Greek island, to a lavish event with the Colosseum as a backdrop.

So why do couples elope? An elopement can be the perfect option to say "I Do" without the stress of a full-fledged wedding. Some couples opt out of a big expensive celebration and use the money for an extended honeymoon trip or even the down payment on a house. And many couples prefer the privacy of pledging their love with only a couple of witnesses.

Elopement doesn't have to mean a quick stop at the Justice of the Peace. It can be a simple yet elegant ceremony in a clergyman's study or a romantic getaway to an exotic destination. Imagine just the two of you exchanging vows on an empty beach.

Every couple is unique, and every elopement is different. The important thing is to find a formula that meets your needs and fulfills your dreams.

To help you begin your elopement process, the first step is to fill out the Elopement Questionnaire. It will help you fine tune the details. Head to rochellecheever.com/resources to download.

16

17

THE ELOPEMENT EXPERIENCE

Case study:
Santorini,
Symbolic

Sofia and Kevin

Venue
Andronis Luxury Suites (ceremony),
around Oia/waterfront for the photos, Oia,
Santorini, Greece

Wedding Planner
DIY

Gown Designer
THEIA

Groom's Clothing Designer
Brooks Brothers

Jewelry/Rings designer
Fuenfer Jewelers for the rings, the brides's
necklace and sapphire ring belonged to her
late grandmother, Anne.

Florist
Betty's flowers, Santorini

19

What inspired you to choose a destination elopement?

Even before we got engaged, we discussed eventually wanting to get married outside of the US. Our families are so spread out with his in Chicago and my family in both California and New York City, so choosing a location and asking all of our family and close friends to travel for a ceremony wasn't something that we wanted to do. We had originally talked about getting married in Italy as my family is Italian – but Kevin's brother and sister-in-law were married in Italy. (Also photographed by Rochelle.) We wanted to do something uniquely us, and because we love to travel, we picked Greece. Kevin had never been and I had only been on a budget Greece trip with some girlfriends from college...very different

In what ways did you personalize your wedding day?

We very much did not want a "cookie-cutter" day/elopement. We wanted it to be very relaxed and low-key and really just a celebration of our union. We went on a 13 mile hike the morning of our wedding, which was a great idea to get rid of any wedding day jitters. For the ceremony, I wore very simple jewelry, just my late grandmother Anne's simple gold necklace and her sapphire ring. It was no frills but that's exactly what we wanted. We had no distractions.

What were your favorite wedding day details?

I absolutely loved my bouquet. I actually brought it to the next two stops and was planning on drying it and bringing it home but it unfortunately didn't hold up after a week of traveling. I loved the simplicity of what both of us wore. Aside from our vows, my favorite part of the day was exploring Santorini and taking photographs. It was my favorite part of the day.

Was there a particular inspiration or theme behind your elopement?
I was inspired by the neutral colors in Santorini. You see a lot of white and blue but then there's the occasional pop of bright pink flowers or a red or green door. I didn't want what we were wearing to be the focus in our photos which is why I chose an ivory dress for me and white pants and a tan linen jacket for Kevin. I wanted a Grecian, flowing dress that felt natural amongst the scenery. I love all things rustic but still elegant and chic.

I wanted flowers that were natural to the region, and neutral in color. We had a lot of white, blush pink, light green, some light yellow in the bouquet. We both wanted to have the ceremony in a location that was representative of Santorini. What better place than a cliff with a view of the Kaldera? We searched around and found the FABULOUS Andronis Luxury Suites. They allowed us to get married on their private terrace and it was magical. I was originally inspired by my sister-in-law's dress which was simple and elegant. I went with a similar theme and got the Theia "Daria" dress which was quite fitted, had a beautiful back detail, and a long train.

Do you have any special advice to share with other brides?
It's hard to plan for a destination elopement, so try to be flexible prior to arrival. You will have an incredibly special day even if not everything goes 100% according to plan. Focus on the union and the significance of the day, rather than the tiny details that you won't remember a year or even a week later.

Chapter 2

Different Types Of Ceremonies

———

ROCHELLE CHEEVER

23

Civil, Religious or Symbolic

There are three types of ceremonies you can choose from for your elopement: Civil, Religious and Symbolic. Every country has its own rules, which can change from city to city, along with the required paperwork. If you want a civil wedding, then I highly suggest contacting your local authorities and the country where you want to get married. Here are some examples of ceremonies I've photographed, which will help you get started with your own ideas.

CIVIL

The process of a legal ceremony depends on the laws of the place in which you want to marry and your nationality. Some countries, such as France, require that you live there for at least 40 days and have residency. In most cases, you will have to have your ceremony at the local town hall.

If you choose to have a civil ceremony abroad, I highly recommend hiring a local wedding planner who knows the language and laws and can help you with the paper work.

24

RELIGIOUS

If you wish to have a religious ceremony abroad, you should first speak to the local clergy about any requirements. They might even suggest a church of your denomination in the area.

The paper work will depend on the venue and its popularity. If you wish to get married in Saint Peter's Basilica, you should prepare a good year in advance. Yes, you really can get married in Saint Peters!

Again, I highly suggest hiring a local wedding planner to help you with the paper work. The bureaucracy in a foreign country can be a headache.

SYMBOLIC CEREMONY

The easiest wedding ceremony to pull off anywhere in the world is a symbolic one. There are no limits to the venue, from a park, a hill-cliff to a beach to an ancient castle. You can rent a romantic apartment or villa with a panoramic terrace to exchange your vows. Or if you prefer, reserve an exotic hotel.

You'll run into just a few restrictions. Some locations require a photo permit, while others don't. If you are a guest most hotels will permit you to take photos there.You may want to ask the photographer to stand back and shoot from a distance, so you won't have the feeling of being watched, and can privately promise your lives to one another, but still have a record of the occasion.

The ceremony can be instead of, or in addition to a a legal exchange of vows. If you choose to get married in a foreign country, a symbolic ceremony may be the best option, since you would otherwise need residency to get a marriage license. Many couples choose a quick and quiet civil ceremony then throw a fantastic destination wedding anywhere in the world.

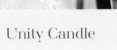

Sand Ceremony

Unity Candle

Wine Ceremony

Sand Ceremony

This is a very simple yet powerful ritual. It involves several jars of sand, each in a different color, which are blended together in a central jar, creating a unique layered design, a symbol of the blending of two lives, which is then given a special place at home. The bride and groom take turns pouring colored sand into the jar, creating a layered effect. Some couples ask the celebrant to add alternating layers of white sand, representing God, the universe or a holy spirit. Other couples use sand from a beach that has particular meaning for them.

Choose colors that symbolize each of you, her shades reflecting her own personality, his shades particular to him. Think of the harmony when layered.

Unity Candle

In this ceremony the bride and groom each have a special candle which they light individually, and then use those two candles to light a third candle, symbolizing the unity of two flames becoming one.

For this ceremony you'll want to find especially beautiful candles that have special meaning for both of you.

Wine Ceremony

The bride and groom drink separately from two chalices, then pour the remaining wine into a third cup and drink from that together, symbolizing the cup of life and the experiences they will share throughout their lives.

For this ceremony it's lovely to bring along special heirloom glasses or goblets.

Case study:
Chianti, Tuscany
Civil

Tania and Chris

Venue
Castellina in Chianti

Gown Designer
Luna Novias

Groom's Clothing Designer
Burberry

Shoe designer
Christian Louboutin and To Boot New York

Jewelry/Rings designer
Verragio engagement
and custom wedding bands

Florist
Local florist in Castellina

Hair and makeup Artist
The bride

Catering/Restaurant
L'albergaccio di Castellina

Invitations
Wedding Paper Divas

What inspired you to choose to do a destination elopement?

We wanted the day to be about our marriage, and not whether everyone is having fun at our wedding.
Chris is a certified Master Sommelier and proposed to me in Napa Valley, California. Since we are both fans of
Italian wine, we decided that we should get married in Italy and complete the circle. We planned to elope from the
very beginning, and Castellina met our requirements of serenity, privacy, and a soothing atmosphere with Italian charm.
We couldn't be happier with our little town.

In what ways did you personalize your wedding day?

It was a huge deal for me to match our wedding certificate and our actual wedding date. We wanted our elopement to be
the day we get married, and not us dressing up for photos. It was a lot of hard work, but we chose to get legally married in
Italy and own an Italian marriage license. We didn't think too much on the details. Most of our stress came from finalizing
the legal side. We chose a simple postcard for our elopement announcements. I found a dress that I was able to move in
comfortably around town. The flowers were bought the night before the wedding at a local shop near the castle. The venue
was chosen because it was bare and seemed untouched. Everything was really natural looking and romantic.

What were your favorite wedding day details?
I loved so many things from this day! Because we ran away, it made the day our little secret. My absolute favorite part is the first look. My husband carried my garment bag through our travels without peeking to see the dress. The expression on his face helped me remember the reason we were getting married.

Was there a particular inspiration or theme behind your elopement?
The theme for the day was natural. We didn't want it to be stuffy or fancy. Italy is so relaxed and go-with-the-flow that we didn't want to look done. He wore a suit, instead of a tux. I had my hair flowing with natural makeup. We both looked like ourselves.

Do you have any special advice to share with other brides?
I didn't realize how important this was until the day of the wedding. It is very important that you get a photographer that speaks your language. Rochelle understood what we wanted and helped us navigate around town for photos. Also, I can't help but recommend an elopement. A wedding in your home country is stressful enough, but imagine planning it from across the ocean. As for getting it legally recognized, be sure to do lots of research in advance.

31

Chapter 3

DIY or Wedding Planner

ROCHELLE CHEEVER

33

DIY or Wedding Planner

If you decide to have a civil or religious ceremony at a foreign destination, I recommend hiring a wedding planner, at least for the paperwork. I've seen all sorts of combinations, from brides who wanted to design everything from the dress, to the invites, venue, and ceremony. The five elopements below are some examples of who had a DIY and who hired a wedding planner.

DIY

Positano Elopement (Symbolic)– Lindsay and Harsh

After speaking to Lindsay via Skype and getting to know her a bit better, I gave her referrals for a local celebrant, a florist, makeup artist/hair stylist and a boat. Lindsay contacted all the vendors directly herself. She found a stunning venue online and arranged for all the rest. I helped with the timeline for good light (Positano is pretty particular with good light) and her newlywed photographic itinerary.

Rome Elopement (Religious) Dave and Cassie

For this elopement, Cassie contacted an American Church in Rome

Cassie contacted Saint Patrick's Church and the local Pastor helped them organize their wedding. She did her hair and makeup. I helped organize the car and driver around Rome for their newlywed photographs. Please note for all couples who want to elope to Rome, if you want to go around Rome for your newlywed photographs, you need a driver who has a license to drive through the ancient city.

To decide whether you want a do-it-yourself wedding or a wedding planner, ask yourself how much you'll enjoy designing your ceremony. Some brides just want to show up on their wedding day, while others enjoy creating it all themselves. Symbolic weddings are just that, so you can create any ceremony you like. But a wedding planner is a must if you decide on a civil or religious wedding. There's a lot of bureaucracy involved, and it's much easier if you use a professional who knows the ropes and speaks the language.

Another deciding factor is just how plush you want your wedding to be. Do you want an elaborate dinner with flower arrangements? Do you want calligraphy vows, table settings? The more complex, the more you're likely to need a wedding planner.

ROCHELLE CHEEVER

35

ROCHELLE CHEEVER

36

WEDDING PLANNER

Lake Como Elopement (Civil) – Stacey and Shane

For Stacey and Shane's intimate elopement, the bride emailed me inquiring about eloping in Italy. After getting to know her a bit, I had her look at various venues, and she picked Villa Balbianello on Lake Como. She wanted a symbolic wedding since she'd decided to have a civil wedding back home. Stacey wanted a wedding planner to help her with booking the villa, the boat, flowers, makeup, cake, and dinner. The works. I connected her with a planner in Milan who knows Lake Como very well and took care of everything, even helping with timeline and newlywed itinerary.

Orvieto Elopement (civil) - La Badia - Christie and Darren

The bride contacted me, and I helped her connect with a wedding planner. Christie just wanted to show up on her wedding day and have everything ready, so the wedding planner took care of it all for her. She booked La Badia, the City hall in Orvieto, a spectacular former 12th-Century Benedictine abbey, as well as the hair and flowers. I was in the loop to help out with the photographic itinerary for the best light.

37

Case study:
Orvieto,
Civil

Christie and Darren

Location
Orvieto, Italy

Venue
La Badia/ Teatro Mancinelli/ Orvieto

Wedding Planner
Italia Celebrations, Brenda and Chiara

Gown Designer
BHLDN, Badgley Mischka

Shoe designer
Kate Spade

Florist
Noosheen's Floral Event Design

38

39

What inspired you to choose a destination wedding?

Getting married in Europe first started out as a joke. Once I did a little research I saw that legally it would be possible to get married in Italy with their favorable residency requirements. Then, Darren challenged me to find a way to get married—he gave me till the end of the month. By the end of the week I figured it out! In a large part thanks to Rochelle! She put us in touch with Brenda and Italia Celebrations. At first it seemed difficult to get married in Italy with some of the legal requirements and paperwork, but with their help, it quickly became apparent that it would not only be easy but it was also reasonable.

When Darren and I talked about getting married, we never wanted something big or over-the-top. We wanted something very special, unique, and small. We did not want to be overwhelmed on our special day and really wanted it to be just about him and me! When we saw the idea of an Italian wedding/elopement take shape, we knew it was the perfect place. Initially we were supposed to get married in Rome, but due to Rome's Birthday, we relocated the wedding to Orvieto! That was the best "hiccup" that happened during the planning stages. The more we researched Orvieto, the more we knew it was the perfect fit for what we wanted.

In what ways did you personalize your wedding day?

I would say the whole day was personalized for us. Chiara and Brenda did a great job making sure every detail was perfect. Because it was so small (5 guests) we felt like the whole day was just about us!

What were your favorite wedding day details?

Our favorite wedding day detail was the lace at the edge of my veil. It was the lace from Darren's mom's wedding dress— about 45 old. We lost Darren's mom in January 2015. It was important to us that she was with us in some way on the day we were married. I racked my head trying to figure how we would honor her in a meaningful way. She was Darren's best friend and I wanted her memory to be honored. One day I was looking at a picture of her wedding dress and it dawned on me that the lace would be a perfect border for my veil! After getting permission from Darren and his brother, I cut the bottom layer of her wedding dress to retrieve enough lace. I found a wonderful seamstress on Etsy.com who understood my vision and appreciated the memory I was trying to honor. I sent the lace to a stranger in Oklahoma and six weeks later she sent me the finished product. It wasn't until after I purchased my wedding dress that I was able to see how the dress and the veil worked together. In fact, the dress was already halfway through the alteration process when I first tried them both on together. I felt in my heart that I was wearing the ensemble for the day I would be married. The veil completed and complimented the dress so well! I was overcome with emotion and so pleased with the end result.

Another favorite wedding day detail were my shoes! Anyone who knows me, knows how much I love Kate Spade. At the advice of a good friend, I decided that I would wear a wedge. I scoured the internet for the perfect wedding day wedge and I finally found it on katespade.com.

I also loved the blue Tiffany's heart pendant Darren gave me in Rome, the day before we got married. He knew I had forgotten my "something" blue and he saved the day! I pinned the pendant with a safety pin inside my dress over my heart.

Was there a particular inspiration or theme behind your wedding?

For the flowers I wanted the colors to be light and pastel. Darren's mom, Roda, loved light pinks, purples, blues and other pastels. Again, I wanted her to be a part of the day and asked that my bouquet have some of those colors.

For my dress I wanted something simple, elegant, and timeless. I did not want something trendy that I would regret 15-20 years from now....like the big puffy sleeves of the 80s and 90s. I also did not want a big ball gown, puffy dress. In fact, I had the belt sewn onto the dress and the train cut off because it was too much of a hassle to keep fixing them.

My best friend showed me the beautiful gowns that BHLDN had to offer. I fell in love with the variety of styles and the prices! I did not want to spend a fortune, but I also wanted to love the dress I would be wearing. I immediately loved athe Livia Gown and pinned it to my Pintrest page. I made an appointment at the BHLDN in Beverly Hills. The Livia was the first gown I tried on, because I was so excited to see how it would look on me. I tried on four other dresses that day but I always went back to the Livia Gown. My assigned "stylist" at BHLDN paired it with the gorgeous Calla Sash belt and a veil. Immediately I knew this was my look and dress, but I needed to think about it over lunch. After having lunch down the street, I went back to BHLDN and ended up buying the Livia Gown and the last Calla Sash that the entire BHLDN online store had in stock.

Darren did not see my dress until our first look. I wanted to keep it a surprise and I had him convinced it was a shorter dress. Ultimately, he loved the dress that I wore!

Do you have any special advice to share with other brides?

Having such a small wedding/elopement I felt like I was really able to enjoy each minute of the day. I made a point to try to savor everything and commit it to memory. I felt it was easy to do because I was in great hands with Chiara from Italia Celebrations and Rochelle. Having their help, I did not worry about timelines, poses, pictures, etc. I was able to truly just enjoy the day and live in the moment, which was better than I could have imagined, a moment that exceeded all of my expectations, and a moment that I always want to relive.

The moment that I always look back on and the best of the day was our first look. I have played it over in my head, I swear, I have memorized everything prior and during the first look. I remember the excitement of walking from the hotel and seeing Darren standing with his back toward me, waiting for me. As I looked at him waiting for me, I felt a wave of different emotions that I have never experienced. I remember thinking to myself that what I was feeling was happiness, true happiness. I wanted to be in this moment forever. As I walked towards Darren, I knew I was walking to the best man I knew and the man who would make me the happiest person.

Looking back, the way everything worked out seemed like it was all meant to be. The town of Orvieto was a pleasant surprise. The people were so friendly and welcoming. It made the day feel even more personal and special. We always look back on that day and are overcome with the town's beauty and the kindness of all its citizens. We were so lucky to get married in Orvieto. It will always have a special place in our hearts. We will be sure to return!

41

Where to Elope

Where to Elope

For your happily ever after, probably the first (and most fun) thing to do is to choose a place that is meaningful to both of you. Years ago, elopements used to mean secretly running away to Las Vegas and getting married in a cheesy wedding chapel. Nowadays, the options are endless. You can live your dream elopement and why not even dream a little bigger? Make it a trip of a lifetime and include your dream honeymoon, too! The sky is the limit.

An Elopement can be an incredibly romantic way of declaring your love to each other No need to worry about guest lists, seating plans, arguing over wedding invitations and flower arrangements. You can even skip the significant wedding stress and run away to someplace exotic and beautiful.

So where? The world is open, and the choice is yours. To start generating ideas, pick a location that has had a significant impact on your relationship, like where you met or where you had your first date or where he proposed. Begin by asking yourselves these questions:

- Is there a place that is meaningful to you both?
- Are you dreaming of visiting a foreign country?
- Are you adventurous? Do you love to hike?
- Do you like warm weather or maybe someplace cool like the Dolomites, Lake Geneva, Switzerland or Iceland?
- Do you love cliff views or ocean views, green gardens or dramatic landscapes?
- Do you prefer the countryside, quaint towns or historic cities?
- Do you love art? Food? What type of food?
- Are you a wine connoisseur?

44

1. Rome

What I love:

✦ Artistic and Architectural backdrops

✦ History

✦ Good food & wine

✦ Very romantic

✦ Chic

✦ Beautiful churches

✦ Statues

✦ Colors - earth tones, ochres and reds

✦ Ancient ruins

BEST TIME OF THE YEAR: APRIL, MAY, SEPT, OCTOBER

2. Santorini

What I love:

✦ Amazing backdrops of the Aegean Sea

✦ Colors - white & blue with pastels

✦ Unique architecture

✦ Great food and hospitality

✦ Quaint Island

BEST TIME OF THE YEAR: APRIL, MAY, SEPT, OCTOBER

ROCHELLE CHEEVER

45

3. Mexico - Punta Mita /Sayulita/ Cabo San Lucas / Tulum

What I love:

✦ Unique art

✦ Strong culture

✦ Beautiful beaches

✦ Very colorful

✦ Beautiful Architecture

✦ Great food

BEST TIME OF YEAR: DECEMBER- APRIL

4. Kauai

What I love:

✦ Far from everything

✦ Friendly people

✦ Very laid back

✦ Surfer haven

✦ Beautiful beaches

✦ Nature is unique

✦ Mountains are amazing and look sculpted

✦ Mythology

BEST TIME OF THE YEAR: SEPTEMBER- NOVEMBER | APRIL – JUNE

46

5. Venice

What I love:

+ Very Romantic
+ Quaint
+ Stunning architectural backdrops
+ Food
+ Culture
+ Bridges (over 400)
+ Canals
+ Pastel colors
+ Culture

BEST TIME OF THE YEAR: APRIL, MAY, SEPT, OCTOBER. AVOID JUNE, JULY, AND AUGUST

6. Amalfi Coast (Positano and Ravello)

What I love:

+ Majestic mountain backdrops
+ Quaint seaside villages
+ Romantic
+ Food (especially seafood, limoncello, mozzarella, and granita)
+ Culture (beautiful ceramics)
+ Colors: Pastels, White & blue and yellow (lemons)

BEST TIME OF THE YEAR: APRIL, MAY, SEPT, OCTOBER. AVOID SUMMER! CROWDED WITH TOO MANY TOURISTS.

ROCHELLE CHEEVER

47

7. Southern California - San Diego, Santa Monica, Beverly Hills, Malibu, Palm Springs and Joshua Tree

What I love:

✦ Amazing seascapes

✦ Beaches

✦ Rocks

✦ Colors

✦ Sunset

✦ Great weather year round

✦ Surfer haven

✦ Nature

BEST TIME OF THE YEAR: GREAT YEAR ROUND

What I love about Palm Springs and Joshua Tree — the desert

✦ Cactus

✦ Warm desert colors

✦ Beautiful cactus blossoms in the Spring

✦ Unique nature

✦ Spectacular mountain backdrops

✦ Palm Springs is very 1970 Hollywood Retro

BEST TIME OF THE YEAR: IT CAN GET VERY HOT IN THE SUMMER, SO AVOID JULY & AUGUST.

8. Tuscany

What I love:

✦ Famous Tuscan rolling hills

✦ Wine territory (my favorite)

✦ Tuscan food

✦ Great hospitality

✦ Lush green, rustic backdrops, vineyards

BEST TIME OF THE YEAR: SEPTEMBER- NOVEMBER | APRIL - JUNE

9. Northern California

What I love:

Big Sur

+ Majestic Mountain backdrops
+ Redwood forests
+ Colors - blues, greens
+ Nature, whale watching
+ Unplugged (minimal Internet)

San Francisco

+ Unique Bridges
+ Rolling hills
+ Artistic
+ Cultural
+ Historic City Hall

+ Metropolitan
+ Carmel/Monterey atmospheric seaside towns
+ Seascapes
+ Nature- seals, otters, sea lions
+ Beaches

BEST TIME OF YEAR: YEAR ROUND, IT CAN GET A BIT COLD IN THE WINTER BUT NOTHING TOO EXTREME

10. Provence, France

What I love:

+ Magnificent lavender fields
+ Acres of sunflowers
+ Laid back
+ Artistic
+ Quaint towns
+ Romantic lifestyle
+ Great food

BEST TIME OF YEAR: APRIL, MAY, JUNE, SEPT, OCTOBER. THE LAVENDER BLOOMS IN APRIL AND MAY.

Case Study:
Lake Como,
Symbolic

Stacey and Shane

Venue
Villa del Balbianello

Wedding Planner
Alessia from White Emotion

Gown Designer
Monique Sandoval from
Cleo and Clementine

Groom's Clothing Designer
Ben Sherman

Catering/Restaurant
La Darsena

Shoe designer
Prada for Shane and ASOS for Stacey

Jewelry/Rings designer
Antique rings purchased from Goldadore

Florist
Vertuani Floral Designer

Hair
Caprani Nicoletta

ROCHELLE CHEEVER

51

What inspired you to choose to do a destination wedding in Italy?

We knew we wanted to elope in Europe, but our options were overwhelming! Italy held the most gorgeous views and romance for our dream day. We decided to look for destination photographers first, then stumbled upon Rochelle Cheever. We immediately knew she was the one for us. Her lighting was impeccable and her ability to capture wide scenic views, while still making the couples the star focus sealed the deal! When we saw a photo set she did at Villa del Balbianello with Sing-pey and Michael, we fell in love and wanted to wed at the same place!

In what ways did you personalize your wedding day?

To personalize our day, we picked several small packable items that carried a lot of meaning. My grandmother Grace passed during my childhood, but the love and inspiration she gave me lives on. I wanted to bring her with me and represent her, so I wore her earrings and packed two of her old china plates to use for our wedding cake. I was also able to wear my Great Grandmother Jenny's pearl ring that was passed down four generations. Shane's personalization resonated much deeper meaning for his mother that passed away from breast cancer in 2008. He wore pins on his suit to represent his mom. The paper crane for those they crafted together and a Bruce Springsteen pin because they always listened to him together.

We also had a beautiful ring box made from a Snappy Gum Eucalyptus tree hand-crafted from an Australian artist, Brandi on Etsy. We knew we could admire the box for years to come, reminding us of our special day.

Lastly, we wrote our own vows. Shane and I are quite quirky and part of our bond is based on our humor. There was no other way for us to marry, without doing so in our own words!

What were your favorite wedding day details?

How could it not be the stunning views from Balbianello? I had anticipated our wedding day for months, but it never felt real until we were actually there! The photos you see are stunning, but actually being there brings a magic you can't describe. A detail, very dear to me happened in the very beginning! When we arrived, we were located at the dock at the bottom of the hill of Villa del Balbianello. There was a winding gravel pathway that traveled up and circled around the hill to the top terrace where we'd say our vows. There were some tourists on the grounds below and when they saw that I was in a wedding dress, they all stepped off of the pathway and allowed us to walk ahead, smiling and saying Congratulations. In that moment I felt so special, like Cinderella, or the bride I never envisioned myself to be.

Inspiration/theme behind the day?

Our inspiration was just making the day feel genuine for us. We are a relaxed and goofy couple, so wanted to ensure we could laugh, sing and dance if we wanted to, which we did. We also wanted to allow the theme to be Lake Como, because that was our dream and all we needed for a backdrop.

Tell us a little bit about how you chose your invitations, flowers, venue, and dress?

Villa del Balbianello is the dreamiest location. The views are incredible looking across Lake Como from the top. The grounds are lush, covered with spectacular landscaping. There's gorgeous towering firs, enormous canopy trees, an abundance of flowers and extraordinary vines wrapping around the archways. Every small detail of the villa's architecture holds timeless beauty. It's a location that speaks for itself, without need for any decorations. That's how we knew it was perfect for our elopement.

The dress was quite a quest! I left so many boutiques empty handed. I wanted a dress that felt timeless, but also had some non-traditional components. The only way to de-traditionalize a dress at the store was to order it in champagne or have it tea-length, which wasn't the direction I wanted. I began hunting online, then found Cleo and Clementine. They use modern elements, like leather bodices and alternative colors. Then, they perfectly balance the designs with gorgeous delicate and billowy skirts. My gown had an ivory sweetheart leather bodice, which was excellent for support for a larger bust! The empire waistband was made of silk, and then the skirt was crafted of pink and champagne tulle. To add additional color, peeking through the sheer tulle was a pink ombre' silk charmeuse layer.

The most beloved part of the dress was the lace applique overlay that my mother made for me. I wanted sleeves, but didn't want a standard lace bolero. My mom wanted to create something special for me, so she made a sheer top that I was able to model as she placed each applique in the perfect place. She then hand sewed each individual piece on. It turned out beautiful! I'm so proud of her touch, it will always be the most precious piece I had with me on that day.

52

Overall, do you have any special advice you would like to share with other brides to help prepare them for their destination wedding?

If you hire an experienced wedding planner and wedding photographer, you can take comfort in their expertise. We had never traveled out of the country and were intimidated to plan the day. I couldn't imagine finding a florist, transportation, a bakery, hair stylist or even photo locations. I was able to voice my vision, but then didn't have to worry about making it come to fruition. I truly felt like Rochelle and Alessia carried me through the day like family. It all went flawlessly. I even tripped once tearing part of my dress! It didn't affect anything. So much stress of weddings involves all of the details and expectations, versus the true reason for the day, your fiancé. My advice for other brides is to remember, the day will be perfect no matter what happens, rain or shine because of whom you're with.

We would love to hear how you met, or how you got engaged.

Shane proposed to me right before Christmas. Each year, we took Christmas photos in our hometown by a large Christmas tree in the city center. He wisely knew I'd be appreciative of being dolled up for the occasion and managed to catch the proposal on camera. We were standing by the Christmas tree with our camera on a tripod, ready to take our annual photos and then Shane got down on one knee and surprised me! It was the sweetest thing ever. I can't wait to do photos again this year as husband and wife!

53

When to elope

55

THE ELOPEMENT EXPERIENCE

When to elope

Your first considerations will be finding a time when you are both free from work and family obligations. For a destination elopement, you may want to take as much time as possible, so that you can combine your elopement with a honeymoon — ideally, you'll want at least two weeks.

If you are planning to elope to a popular travel destination such as Rome, Paris, or the Greek island of Santorini, you'll be well-advised to avoid the height of the tourist season, when you'll pay high-season prices, and be faced with crowds.

To help you plan your elopement, I've created this mini-guide to the ideal months for some of my favorite elopement destinations. Consider the list as a starting point for generating ideas, looking at the when and the where for a perfect match. At this point, your choices are unlimited. If you already have an idea of the month you'll be available, start there and see if any of the destinations speak to you. Or start with some of the ideas you've already been dreaming about. If your heart is set on a beach wedding, you have a wide selection to consider, depending on the time of year, from California to Thailand to South Africa and the Bahamas, so the months when you're available will help define your destination choice.

JANUARY & FEBRUARY	MARCH	MARCH
+ Southern California	+ California	+ Joshua Tree (wildflowers)
+ Costa Rica	+ Joshua Tree (cactus wildflowers)	+ Big Sur
+ Kauai	+ Palm Springs	+ Rome
+ Mexico	+ Mexico	+ Amalfi Coast
+ Burger	+ Maldives	+ Greece
+ Bahama	+ Bremuda	+ Southern California
+ Venice	+ Sedona	+ Utah
+ Belize	+ Canary Island	+ Arizona
+ Thailand		+ Japan (Cherry blossoms)
+ South Africa		+ Paris
		+ Cuba
		+ Marrakesh
		+ Switerland

56

APRIL

+ Joshua Tree (wildflowers)
+ Big Sur
+ Rome
+ Amalfi Coast
+ Greece
+ Southern California
+ Utah
+ Arizona
+ Japan (Cherry blossoms)
+ Paris
+ Cuba
+ Marrakesh
+ Switerland

MAY

+ Hawaii
+ California
+ Italy (all)
+ France
+ Greece
+ Utah
+ Yosemite

JUNE

+ Maldives
+ Bali
+ Iceland
+ Croatia
+ Montenegro

JULY & AUGUST

+ Bali
+ Iceland
+ San Diego
+ Seyshells
+ Thailand
+ Portugal
+ Puglia
+ Tuscany
+ Amsterdam
+ Corsica
+ Sardinia

SEPTEMBER

+ Italy(all)
+ Greece
+ California
+ Yosemite
+ Utah
+ Barcelona
+ Spain
+ Zimbabwe

OCTOBER

+ Spain
+ Italy
+ France
+ Greece
+ Rome
+ Florence
+ Venice

NOVEMBER

+ November
+ Morocco
+ California
+ Kauai
+ Grand canyon , Arizona
+ Palm Springs
+ New Zealand
+ Nepal

NOVEMBER

+ St. Barts
+ Southern California (looking for some sun)

For snow lovers:

+ Prague
+ Berlin
+ Zermatt
+ Dolomites

Case Study:
San Diego,
California
Symbolic

McKenna and Garrett

Venue
Rancho Valencia Resort and Spa

Wedding Planner
Francine Ribeau Events

Gown Designer
The Dress Theory

Hair and make-up
Beauty by Stacey

Stationary
Lynn and Lou Paper Co.

Rentals and decor
Folklore Rentals

Cake and desserts
Hey There, Cupcake

Florist
Blooms by Breesa Lee

Video
SJ Videography

59

60

What inspired you to choose to do a destination wedding?

Garrett is from Chicago and I'm from Boston, but we both live and work in Los Angeles. We wanted a winter wedding, because it was easy for both of us to take time off in January, when business is slow. We went down to Rancho Valencia for a weekend getaway and realized it was our perfect wedding location. On impulse, we had eloped at the L.A. City Hall months before, but it was our secret. Only our parents knew about it. Now that we had settled down, we wanted to have a real ceremony and send out announcements. January was the best month for Garrett and me. Business was slow after the holidays so we could easily take a few days off for a mini-honeymoon after the wedding. And our out-of-town guests would be able to get great flights. We'd be at Rancho Valencia off-season so the resort would be very peaceful, but the weather would still be warm and glorious. We were able to book a bungalow suite —just beautiful — for ourselves, and casitas for our guests. We all spent the day before the wedding getting pampered at the spa, where we were scrubbed, steamed and massaged into total relaxation. The morning of our wedding, Garrett and I were still glowing! After the wedding, we drove over the border to Mexico for a secluded honeymoon in a gorgeous house we rented with views of the Pacific.

In what ways did you personalize your wedding day?

We wanted to be sensitive about the way in which we let friends and relatives know that we had decided to go for it and tie the knot. It was important to me that the cards we sent were very personal, in a style that reflected us, and I wanted them to have a touch of luxury about them, so that it was almost as though we were sending little gifts. Our wedding planner suggested Lynn and Lou Paper. Their selection of papers was perfect, and we were able to personalize every aspect of the cards we sent out.

What were your favorite wedding day details?

Rancho Valencia has expansive grounds - 45 magnificently landscaped acres. Thick clusters of flowers bloom in riotous colors all year long. For our wedding, the florist used similar flowers echoing the colors of the grounds — for my bouquet, for the lavish table decoration and in pots of flowers that flanked the spot where we performed the ceremony.

Do you have any special advice to share with other brides?

At first I thought that since we were planning such a simple wedding, with just a few guests in a resort that seemed to have everything, I could organize everything on my own.. But I soon realized that the demands of my job and the leisure hours I wanted to spend with Garret, left me no time. I didn't know where to begin sourcing vendors in San Diego and I didn't have the patience to do an extensive Internet search. Francine did everything for me. I just chose my dress, packed my bag and showed up at the resort.

Chapter 6

Inspirational Image Board

ROCHELLE CHEEVER

63

Create an Inspirational Image Board

To help you fine tune your elopement and make it "yours" I suggest creating an Inspirational Image Board using Pinterest to generate ideas. Ideally, you should create a new account just for your elopement and use a different email address to set up your Pinterest elopement profie. If you prefer, make several new boards on your own Pinterest page.

1. ENVIRONMENT

The most important board to start with is the place or the environment. It's the biggest decision you'll make and once you have it nailed, you can work on the overall mood, your attire, color scheme and flowers. It can be venue such as a hotel or restaurant, or a Hawaiian beach, Yosemite or the Swiss Alps. Think big and have fun.

2. MOOD

Sit down with your fiancé and choose a few adjectives to describe yourselves and then the mood of your wedding. Try to choose a few adjectives that reflect your own personalities. Some ideas: romantic, adventurous, playful, colorful.

For more ideas, please check the Mood Adjective Board in this chapter.

3. FIRST BOARD

Create your first board and call it ENVIRONMENT. If you are adding this new board to your own Pinterest account you might want to call it ELOPEMENT_ENVIRONMENT.

4. KEYWORDS

To narrow down your search in Pinterest, type in your keywords along with one or two adjectives: elopement, beach or elopement, adventurous. When you find something that speaks to you, add it to your ENVIRONMENT board.

5. FAVORITES

Choose about 10 of your favorites and add a description as to why you like each one.

6. NAME YOUR BOARDS

With the environment as your main inspiration, create the other boards that are important to you (color, overall look, mood).

a. Overleaf are some ideas for other boards: (Try to stick to no more than 10 to avoid overload.)

64

- Venue
- Color Scheme
- Type of Ceremony
- Reception
- Food
- Music
- Invites
- Gown
- Shoes
- Hair
- Makeup
- Accessories (dogs, instruments etc.)

If you are using your own Pinterest account, then label each new board something like this:
- ELOPE_venue
- ELOPE_gown
- ELOPE_color scheme

7. BRAINSTORM

This is when you start to generate your own ideas. Begin to follow boards and collect pins. Use the Pinterest search bar if needed. Dump everything you like onto the appropriate board and brainstorm. This stage should take at least a few days to about a week. It's good to sleep on your ideas and think about them, returning with a fresh eye each day. Delete the ones you don't like or select favorites.

8. FINAL BOARD

When your vision starts to take shape, create your last board:
- ELOPEMENT_Final mood

9. NARROW DOWN

Go back to all your boards and select your favorites from each board about 2-3 pins per board. You need to narrow down all your images to a total of about 20-30.

10. CLARITY

And voila'! By now you should have a clear idea of your overall elopement and how you envision it.

11. SHARE

You can share your final board with your wedding planner, send it to your make-up and hair stylists...and it should help you with all your decisions. If you are doing the elopement DIY, you can reach out to venues and check their availability. You can also add my Pinterest handle as well as I have a lot of great ideas (Rochelle Cheever).

Add collaborators by clicking the plus sign. A designer tip: Try to keep colors to no more than three harmonious shades in order to have a cohesive look.

65

Mood Adjective Sheet

- bold
- conservative
- timid
- passionate
- peaceful
- quiet
- unique
- romantic
- energetic
- loud
- passionate
- colorful
- calm
- soft pastels
- courageous
- timeless
- classical
- joyful
- powerful
- vivacious
- reserved
- soft
- introverted
- extroverted
- physical

- lively
- thoughtful
- moody
- down to earth
- understanding
- charismatic
- chic
- beautiful
- strength
- considerate
- sophisticated
- humble
- lavish
- artistic
- authentic
- delicate
- modest
- gregarious
- sociable
- stable
- kind
- loving
- agreeable
- analytical
- assertive

- patient
- clumsy
- emotional
- sentimental
- reliable
- natural
- ambitious
- sensual
- versatile playful artistic
- industrious talkative subtle
- balanced
- flexible
- flowing
- fleshy
- delicate
- adventurous
- whimsical
- chivalrous
- enchanting
- loving
- picturesque
- poetic
- idyllic

66

THE ELOPEMENT EXPERIENCE

Case study:
Rome,
Symbolic

Heidi and Michael

Venues
La Posta Vecchia/ Sant'Anna Chapel,
the Vatican

Wedding Planner
Martina Coppino

Gown Designer
Lavendar Bridal

Groom's Clothing Designer
Hart Schaffner & Marx

Makeup
La Posta Vecchia Beauty Club

Shoe designer
Michael Kors

Jewelry/Rings designer
Custom, MK Designs,
Michelle McGuinnes 216-215-5253

Florist
Loreta Fiori, Ladispoli

Hair
Erica Marhofer

69

THE ELOPEMENT EXPERIENCE

Was there a particular inspiration or theme behind your wedding?

Michael and I knew we wanted a very private wedding with only our closest family and we wanted our guests to have a memorable experience – one they would talk about for years to come. Italy, especially Rome, made a stunning setting for our week together. We hired a professional guide to take our families on a panoramic photo tour just before sunset while Rochelle, our wedding photographer, whisked us around Rome taking our photos. We are definitely not the crafty type but Pinterest gave us some great ideas for floral arrangements. I visited blogs such as Grey Likes Weddings and Destination I Do for ideas to customize a color scheme and create check-lists so no detail would be overlooked. I kept it completely simple. My wedding gown was a slip dress in exquisite lace with just a bit of a train so it didn't get in my way later. I had a long veil pinned to the back of my head that trailed behind me as I walked down the aisle. My bridesmaid also wore a long slip dress in a similar style, also in white. We hired a vintage white car for the day to drive from our seaside hotel to the Vatican for the ceremony and back. The flowers were white roses accented by very pale peach roses and my bouquet was in the same pastels. The ceremony was unforgettable because we were in a historic chapel full of art, and we had it all to ourselves. We had a wedding that was uniquely us and one most girls only dream of. The elements of the sea roaring at La Posta Vecchia during our reception and the sunset over Rome in our photos are unprecedented.

What were your favorite wedding day details?

The traditional ceremony was beautiful, surrounded by stunning architecture. The whole day had magical elements —the sea behind us, the sunset — but my favorite detail was when the bandleader, who had been told that my Italian grandfather was a singer, handed him the microphone. He performed a heartwarming solo for us of "That's Amore," in both English and Italian. He really stole the show.

Do you have any special advice to share with other brides?

"Create a timeline that gives you plenty of room for curveballs leading up to and during your day. Interview and select a wedding planner who you can trust to create a smooth, stress-free event and hire the most amazing photographer you can find. Photos are what you will have to share the event with those who were not there and recreate the magic you felt on that day."

Chapter 7

Timeline & Itinerary

ROCHELLE CHEEVER

73

The Perfect Elopement Timeline & Photographic Itinerary

You've booked your date and your venue is confirmed. Congratulations! You've done the hardest part and the rest of the job is fun. The next step is to plan your elopement day timeline. It is a lot easier than a full-fledged wedding, which often can last 12 hours and sometimes even days. UGH! Elopements usually last from about 4-6 hours depending on what you include in your big day.

If good photography is important to you, avoid the mid-day hours, say from 10 am to 2 pm, when the light is harsh. The most romantic light is usually from late afternoon until sunset. Early morning is also beautiful but not many people want to get up at sunrise to get ready then get married, although I've done it in places like Rome or Venice where it can get super crowded in the afternoon.

The first thing to do is to look online at timeanddate.com to find out what time the sun will rise and set on your wedding day in the location you've chosen for your ceremony. Then plan your day around that time.

Personally, I think it's nice to tell the whole story of your day. It doesn't have to be super extensive, which is the great thing about elopements. Short, sweet and fun. You should consider an heirloom album, especially since you are likely to opt for a small to non-existent guest list and you'll want something to show people who weren't at the ceremony.

Head to rochellecheever.com/resources to download my Elopement timeline planner.

1-2 hours – Getting ready or moments before

These are the "before" pictures: the bride and groom getting ready, details (jewelry, invites or whatever is important to you), a few portraits, These final moments are filled with emotion, so you'll want to capture them.

1 hour - Ceremony

A symbolic ceremony is short — about 20 minutes. Civil or religious ceremonies are a bit longer — 30-40 minutes. If you're having guests, you'll want more time to shoot a few group photographs after the ceremony

1-3 hours - Newlywed photographs

With a destination wedding, it's nice to incorporate the location in the photographs. Perhaps the newlyweds strolling through the village, along the beach or in the gardens, using strategic spots as backdrops. Your photographer should know where these are. If you are not planning on a reception or intimate dinner afterwards, why not continue shooting photos into the sunset hours?

3+ hours - Reception

If you are thinking of having an intimate dinner, reception or simply just cake and champagne, then add on at least an hour. You'll want to arrive at the location about ½ to 1 hour before sunset to get some natural light. You can go into the evening but the most magical light is natural light. I've photographed a few elopements with fireworks and if that's part of your plan, add some extra time accordingly. If there's going to be a first dance, you'll want shots of that, as well.

Make a list of all the things you want to include in your elopement and the ideal photographic itinerary for your wedding day. Then add the allotted time. Add a bit more time to each event to allow for travel between locations. You'll want to take it easy and enjoy the moment instead of hurrying from place to place.

Sunset at 8:00 pm, reception (5/6-hour shoot)

3-4 pm	Before the ceremony shots, getting ready.
4-5 pm	Ceremony
5-7 pm	Newlywed photographs
7-8 or 9 pm	Reception

Sunset at 8 pm, no reception (4-hour shoot)

3-4 pm	Before the ceremony shots, getting ready.
4-5 pm	Ceremony and mingling
5-6 pm	Newlywed portraits

ROCHELLE CHEEVER

75

Case study:
Rome, Italy,
Civil

Lea and Nicholas

Venue
Vignola Mattei complex, Baths of Caracalla.
Rome, Italy

Wedding Planner
Daniela De Luca of Dolce Vita Weddings

Gown Designer
Mignonette Bridal

Groom's Clothing Designer
Nicholas Joseph Custom Suits

Hair and Makeup
Mauro Lulli Salon

Shoe designer
Vince Camuto

Jewelry/Rings designer
Rahmanim's Imports

Catering/ Restaurant
La Griffe Ristorante, Roma

Invitations
Jessica Roux

What inspired you to choose to do a destination elopement?

We did a lot thinking, and ultimately what mattered most to us was having a new experience in a new place together to start our marriage. We also love to travel, and this felt like the best excuse to have a trip with everyone we loved. Neither of us had been to Rome, and we'd wanted to go for some time. When we realized it was relatively easy to pull the paperwork together and make this thing legal on an international level, it felt like the perfect way to get married.

In what ways did you personalize your wedding day?

We did what we wanted, how we wanted. We woke up together, had breakfast with our families, and Nick went to get a haircut with his best friend while I got ready. We wrote each other letters, which we read while getting ready, and we both tried to spend as much time with our loved ones on the day as possible. Keeping our family and friends as involved with the getting-ready and ceremony parts of the day, made us feel like we were taking a step with our community around us and kept the event from feeling presentational. I also chose to read one of my most cherished books while I got my hair done, which turned out to be one of my favorite memories from the day; it kept me feeling like myself throughout all the flutter and excitement. Nick spent most of the day with his best friend, which made him feel grounded.

Was there a particular inspiration or theme behind your elopement?

I was heavily influenced by Rochelle Cheever's style, and I knew if I could have her as our photographer the whole feel of the day would be warm and happy, but also classic with a rustic edge. She had done a photo shoot of an elopement in Rome, and I remember thinking, "That's how I want to feel on our wedding day." Since Rome has so many earthy colors, I wanted the colors of the day to really pop against the stoniness of Rome. So I guess Rome and Rochelle were the biggest inspirations! There was also a nod to "bears." Nick is from from Missoula, MT (home of the Grizzlies), loves the football team the Bears, and the animal has become a mascot of our relationship over the years, so we knew they had to be worked into the day. Our invitation ended up having one brown bear and one grizzly on it, and our hashtag was #bearsroamitaly.

I was adamant about doing my own bouquet and boutonnieres because I used to be a florist, so I went to the Campo di Fiori the day before the wedding with my girlfriends and made the bouquet. One of my friends pulled together the boutonnieres in the morning and brought everything over to our hotel room, where I was getting ready. I had brought my own ribbon, floral tape, scissors and pins in my suitcase. We had printed agenda cards ahead of time, and made welcome bags for our guests so they had snacks, pain-killers, wipes for wine-stained teeth and ribbon-wrapped baggies of confetti for the ceremony.

After choosing Rome and knowing we wanted to work with Rochelle, the venue made the biggest impact on the design of the day. There are only three options for a civil hall in Rome, so it was pretty easy! Vignola Mattei is rustic and charming, and it also felt easy and the most "us" of all the civil halls in Rome. Once I knew we'd booked it, the dress was next. When I walked into Mignonette Bridal in Chicago, I immediately knew that K'poene Kofi-Bruce (the owner of Mignonette) was the woman I wanted to work with. She looked at my body, and put me in something structured and sexy, but romantic and easy to move in. K'poene (pronounced "pin-nay") also understood that the dress needed to be easy to travel with. The dress is a two-piece; she custom-built the corset top from scratch for me, and the skirt is a chiffon A-line, both slightly different colors. When she placed a massive ghostly veil on my head it was clear that the dress fit the venue, and the whole day started to come into focus. Since the day was originally going to be an elopement (which transformed into a small destination-wedding) I was looking for elopement announcements rather than invitations. I couldn't find anything I liked, so I started thinking outside the box. I found Jessica Roux's gorgeous work on a wedding website, and immediately contacted her. She was incredibly easy to communicate with, and offered us lots of options. We were very into the idea of paying an artist to create something we could later frame. Jessica created a postcard-style marriage announcement with the invitation for our celebration party (in Chicago) on the back. She also sent us a large version for our home to match all our bear art!

78

What were your favorite wedding day details?

It is so hard to say because everything was perfect! I am so happy that I made my own bouquet, and that all the guests worked with the color scheme. I wanted bright colors, and colors that felt warm and passionate, and looking out at our guests during the ceremony against the red chairs at Vignola Mattei felt like a giant heart beating back at us.

Do you have any special advice to share with other brides?

Get a wedding planner. It's just not practical to try to do everything on your own, across an ocean, with a different time zone, and cultural differences and possibly a foreign language to boot. Daniela of Dolce Vita Weddings was amazing at helping us navigating what needed to be done, and when. I planned 75% of the wedding with her from my work desk, and handled the little bits on my own. The hardest part is the paperwork, so if you can get through that, you're going to be in good shape! Also, make it easy on the guests; choose a place that is easy to get to and has relatively reliable weather.

Have fun and enjoy your day. We extended our whole wedding into a week-long adventure in a city we'd never been to, and it still flew by! Breathe during the ceremony. Eat at the dinner. Drink a cocktail. Save room for cake. Don't feel bad saying "no"; just say it, and move on. You'll save time on the day feeling guilty! As much as we all want an amazing Pinterest and wedding website-worthy wedding, if you focus on how you want to remember the day and the feeling you want to hold on to, how it looked becomes secondary. Nick said it best, "Just marry a badass person."

Chapter 8

The etiquette of eloping

THE ELOPEMENT EXPERIENCE

The Etiquette
of Eloping

Having photographed so many elopements and met so many couples, I really can't say that there is a "correct" way to do it. A lot depends on the couple's culture, religion, upbringing, age, and how close they are to family and friends. Elopement is often a logical choice for a second wedding, especially if one or both people had formal first weddings and want to keep it simple this time around.

Some couples invite their closest friends and immediate family to the elopement, saying, "My mother would have died if we hadn't told her." Other couples elope in complete privacy, and announce their marriage afterwards with a wedding photo. Quite a few couples I've met decided to elope and and used the money they saved for a down payment on a house.

If children are involved, couples often choose to include them. Another option is a simple elopement to a romantic destination followed by a traditional reception for family and friends back home. Couples who have already been living together sometimes feel their decision to be formally married is just for them to know.

If you are wondering how to structure your elopement, ask yourselves if anyone will be offended, and discuss your plans together. Here some of the ways in which I've seen couples elope successfully:

+ A completely secret marriage at a romantic destination, announced only after the bride and groom return home.

+ A private elopement announced immediately after the ceremony through an online photo, message or phone calls.

+ A private ceremony made accessible to friends and family who watch live via Skype or another online service.

+ An elopement ceremony that includes family and friends.

+ An eloquent that includes the couple's children in the ceremony.

+ An elopement that is not secret at all, but announced before the ceremony, conducted with or without guests.

+ A private elopement followed by a traditional reception for family and friends.

83

THE ELOPEMENT EXPERIENCE

Case study:
Puglia, Italy,
Religious

Victoria and Andreas

Venues
Cathedral of Monopoli, I Montili
Borgobianco Resort and Spa

Wedding Planner
Daniela De Luca of Dolce Vita Weddings

Gown Designer
Monique Lhuillier

Bridesmaids' Dresses
Twobirds

Shoes
Jimmy Choo

Makeup Artist
Silvia Gerzeli

THE ELOPEMENT EXPERIENCE

What inspired you to choose to do a destination wedding?

I'm from Sweden and Andreas is from Norway, but we both live and work in Dubai, so it made sense to choose a neutral location for our wedding, so that our families could also enjoy a vacation. We travel a lot, so we've had the chance to visit a number of beautiful places, but nothing compares to the romance of Puglia. The extraordinary, cone-shaped white limestone architecture, the breathtaking Adriatic sea, and the picture-perfect Cathedral of Monopoli combined to make a dreamscape for our wedding.

In what ways did you personalize your wedding day?

The landscape of Puglia is dominated by the white of the tufa rock, which is everywhere, and is used in the trulli, the cone-shaped buildings that have withstood centuries. Even the cathedral is white with a white interior, offset by touches of gold and the blue of the sky. I wanted the theme of our wedding to be joyous, so I added bright touches of color to contrast the clarity of the white. My four bridesmaids each wore a color that would stand out — shades of deep blue and purple. The men in the wedding party wore suits with blue or purple ties and red and pink boutonnières. The flowers were all created in deep, warm reds and purples. After the ceremony, the guests strolled through the historic village to the reception at Montilli, an ancient manor house surrounded my olive groves. We kept the theme going right down to the gold and white place cards and the white wedding cake, which had colorful fresh flowers placed on each layer.

What were your favorite wedding day details?

My father and I arrived at the cathedral in a vintage white roadster convertible. I stepped out of the car with a huge smile on my face!

Do you have any special advice to share with other brides?

This is the most important day of your life. Make it memorable, but make it enjoyable. It's about the two of you and the love you have for each other. Enjoy all the planning, finding a color scheme, choosing the dresses, the menu, but none of that really matters when your wedding day arrives. Just relax and let the day unwind.

ROCHELLE CHEEVER

87

What to Pack for Your Elopement

89

THE ELOPEMENT EXPERIENCE

What to Pack for Your Elopement

If the point of elopement is to avoid stress, then it would make sense to pack light. Still, you are preparing for one of the most important days in your life, so you'll want to make sure you'll have everything you need, and in the excitement of getting ready, you could easily forget something critical. Check these lists before you close your bags!

The most important things should be in your carry on

+ Passports. Be sure they are up to date.

+ Check to sure if you need a visa.

+ If you had a civil wedding back home, will you need to bring the certificate?

+ Any other necessary paperwork?

+ Copies of birth certificates (just in case)

+ Photocopy of all credit cards – just in case you lose them and a list of contact numbers

+ Keep your credit cards in different places. If you lose one, you"ll have a backup.

+ Wedding rings. Keep them on you and don't put them in the suitcase. You could lose the suitcase.

+ Wedding dress, veil, suit, shoes all in a carry on... sometimes you can put them in a suit bag.

+ Plane tickets You can even have a copy of your ticket on your cell phone. Most boarding passes now are available digitally. Be sure you have a photo of the boarding pass on your phone in case you find yourself in a non-Internet zone.

+ Cash in the local currency —enough for the first couple of days.

+ List of all vendor info & contracts

+ Trip insurance

+ Number of the local consulate or embassy in case of an emergency

THE ESSENTIALS

Before you go, check the local electrical voltage and, if necessary, get adapters

Wedding night lingerie

Something old, blue, borrowed

Vows (if you've written your own)

Paper goods (Programs, menu, invitations.) Bring an extra copy to photograph.

If you are doing a sand or unity ceremony, you'll need supplies for that.

Decorations

PERSONAL ITEMS

Glasses	Curling iron or hot roller
Contact lens	Sunblock (if needed)
Sunglasses	Insect repellent (if needed)
Nail scissors	Shaving cream/razor
Nail file	Makeup & make up remover
Tooth brushes & tooth paste	Moisturizer
Hair products	

ELECTRONICS

Camera (plus memory card and charger)

Cell phone & charger (check voltage) You may want to load your phone with music for the trip.

It's usually possible to ship the wedding gown and other items home after the ceremony, so you won't have to lug them around during the honeymoon.

Lingerie	
Summer dresses Or warm jackets if a winter wedding	
Light jacket for cooler weather	
Shoes (one dressy, one comfy for walking) Beware of new shoes. Be sure you break them in before leaving. Nobody wants blisters on their wedding day.	
A hat for sunny climates.	
Bathing suit, cover up and flip flops if it's a tropical trip.	
Outfits. Plan on 2-3 outfits that travel well and can wash easily. Depending on how long you stay, you can either have the hotel do a wash for you or maybe bring a laundry mat. If you are staying at an Airbnb, check that they have a washing machine. It's always more fun to travel with light luggage than to drag around a big bag filled with more options than you need.	
Guides, maps	
Books or load up your Kindle or iPad.	

Extras

✦ Avoid sun tanning at least 2 weeks before your wedding. A tan can ruin the look of your complexion in photos, tending to turn the skin an unhealthy yellow tone. And be careful of tan lines!

✦ Check your cell phone provider and see if they have international travel plans. I personally use T-mobile and it is great in Mexico, Europe and the States. It might be a bit slow in some regions but it's pretty reliable. You can also consider getting a local phone card when abroad.

✦ If you don't have an international plan turn off your data while you are abroad. Again ask your phone provider how and what.

✦ Leave a copy of your passport with someone back home just for extra safety with all the addresses you'll be going to. Tuck another into your suitcase. In case you lose the original, you can take the copy to the local consulate to get an emergency replacement.

THE ELOPEMENT EXPERIENCE

Case study: Ravello, Italy, Symbolic

Randi and Nicholas

Venue
Villa Cimbrone, Ravello, Italy

Gown Designer
Jenny Packham

Groom's Clothing Designer
Giorgio Armani

Florist
Armando Malafronte

Catering/Restaurant
Il Flauto di Pan

Shoe designer
SJP by Sarah Jessica Parker

Jewelry/Rings designer
Albert Albaladejo

Hair Artist
Piero Mansi

Makeup Artist
Nicki Storey

94

ROCHELLE CHEEVER

What inspired you to choose to do a destination elopement?

Deciding to elope wasn't just a financial consideration, though I'd be fibbing if I said that didn't play a role. However, it was financially motivating in a very different way. While we still spent nearly the same amount as the average wedding costs in the United States, we were able to really maximize our dollars. Rather than dump a ton of money into something that only lasted a few hours, we had the freedom to invest in what was most important to us — our marriage.

Most weddings end up being planned in an effort to please everyone else, and the entire purpose of celebrating the couple quickly becomes lost in the fuss. We wanted our wedding to be about us and our love and our lives, not about throwing the best party or bickering with family members over seating arrangements and dinner menus.

Eloping allowed us to book the wedding location of our dreams and make the most incredible memories galavanting around 14 different cities in Italy and enjoying the best accommodations, dining, and entertainment that the most romantic country on earth has to offer. More importantly, it kept things stress-free so that we could focus on what really mattered: our marriage and starting our lives together, truly together, just the two of us.

In what ways did you personalize your wedding day?

Anyone who knows me knows that I have a serious shoe obsession. I LOVE shoes. I was lucky enough to walk down the aisle in a pair signed by Sarah Jessica Parker, who not only played Carrie Bradshaw, a fellow shoe fanatic on Sex and the City, but IS the queen of shoes herself.

What were your favorite wedding day details?

The fact that it was just the two of us, the look on my husband's face as I walked down the aisle was completely unfiltered and you could see the joy just overflowing I don't think he would have let go and shown the same level of emotion if we had an audience of friends and family staring at us.

Was there a particular inspiration or theme behind your elopement?

The origins of the Casciano family can be traced back to San Casciano, Italy – which is a small village outside of Florence. In fact, Nick's grandparents were the most recent generation to be born and live there. The original idea was to become a member of the family in this special town. However, once you discover the beautiful Villa Cimbrone, there's no passing up that venue. We quickly decided to "go big, or go home" and that abandoning San Casciano for those beautiful views was worth it. Tying the knot in the country of Italy was good enough!

Choosing my dress was a classic case of don't try on dresses outside of your price range. I love the glitz and glam of the Roaring 1920s (think of The Great Gatsby) and found that in this Jenny Packham gown at the boutique. Without looking at the price tag I threw it on and instantly fell in love. My best friend started crying, and then the heart attack set in after I saw the cost. Thanks to pre-owned wedding dress websites I was able to locate the same dress in my size for a fraction of the original cost. After some patience and price negotiations with the lovely bride who wore it before me, I was able to own a hand-beaded gown made by a designer who has dressed so many celebrities including the likes of Taylor Swift, Kate Middleton, Blake Lively, Heidi Klum and Angelia Jolie. Wearing something that had that kind of craftsmanship made me feel so incredibly special on my wedding day!

Do you have any special advice to share with other brides?

The biggest help I found was asking my vendors for recommendations on other vendors. Don't try to navigate a million websites on your own – it will be like finding a needle in a haystack. Instead, let the experts who are well-versed in local reputations help you weed out the scams and identify the winners!

ROCHELLE CHEEVER

97

Meet Rochelle Cheever

A fine artist by training, Rochelle studied painting and photography in Washington, D.C. at the Corcoran School of Art. Summers were spent in Italy, poring over, copying, and reinterpreting the works of Leonardo da Vinci and Michelangelo Buonarotti. After a post-graduate stint in portraiture at the Florence Academy of Art, she began to work as a painter, to teach applied art, and to lead workshops.

When she exhibited ten large-scale graphite drawings of her sons in international schools throughout Rome and elsewhere, she began to receive commissions for paintings of children. It's impossible for a small child to sit still and hold a pose, so she prepared by photographing her subjects. Parents, struck by the artistry of these working photographs, asked to purchase them. She was often told that her photographs resembled paintings and that her paintings resembled photographs.

Although she continued to work as a portrait painter, she began to make photographic portraits, as well, realizing that the camera allowed her to capture spontaneity and raw emotion — a smile, a laugh, a fleeting expression. When an American diplomat who saw her portraits asked her to photograph his wedding, she was taken aback, but decided to accept the challenge. To her surprise, she loved the experience of capturing an occasion filled with such joyful emotion. And having spent so many hours before a canvas inside a studio, she welcomed the chance to be on location, out of doors.

Since that first wedding, she has specialized in fine art photographic portraiture, shooting not only weddings, but anniversaries, engagements, vow renewals, proposals — even honeymoons. From photographing children, she had learned to work fast, to capture the unguarded moment, and to approach her subjects with purity and authenticity. She brought these skills to her wedding photography, as well as her skills as a painter, which enabled her to compose compelling images, setting the scene.

She loves the intimacy of elopements, getting to know the couple, the emotion of the most important moment in their lives. For more than a decade, she has worked almost exclusively with couples. Some of them have never been photographed professionally before, and she understands that they might feel super strange and vulnerable in front of the camera, especially as a couple.

But that is her speciality. She knows how to use her camera in a non-invasive way to reveal their authentic selves. Over the years she has developed tons of tricks and tools to help them relax and feel natural. At times, they actually forget that they're being photographed.

Rochelle Cheever has been awarded the Patronage of the Minister of Fine Arts and Culture in Italy (Patroncino del Ministro per i Beni e le Attitvità Culturali), and Artoque (Diploma of Excellence, England). She has been a finalist at the Orvieto International Awards, Lucie International Photography Awards, and Tau Visual (National Association of Professional Photographers of Italy). Her work has been exhibited in Rome at the Vittoriano Museum (with Patronage from the Italian Fine Arts Minister), 100 Artisti a Trastevere, John Cabot University Il Cortile dell'Arte, The American Academy, Explora Museum Italy and at Il Palazzetto Dépendence Hotel Hassler. In Dallas Texas, her work was exhibited at The Fairmont and at the Cattle Baron's Ball.

In the United States of America, her work has been featured in publications such as Style Me Pretty, Strictly Weddings, Destination Inspirations, Junebug Weddings, and the New York Daily News, and in Italy, in publications such as SposaMania, Il Messaggero, Il Giornale, The American and In Rome Now.

Her portraits have been commissioned by the Fendi family, the family of former U.S. Ambassador to Italy Mel Sembler, the Fracassi family, National Geographic CEO David Haslingden and his family; owners of the Energie fashion label the Zansuri Family; Vice-President of Perugia's soccer team Carlo Lancella, former CEO of Colgate-Palmolive in Italy Todd Atwood, and many others.

ROCHELLE
CHEEVER

Find out more about Rochelle and her work at
www.rochellecheever.com and you can email
rochellecheever@gmail.com